Original title:
Joyful Hearts on Christmas Night

Copyright © 2024 Creative Arts Management OÜ
All rights reserved.

Author: Maya Livingston
ISBN HARDBACK: 978-9916-90-976-8
ISBN PAPERBACK: 978-9916-90-977-5

Under the Spell of Twinkling Lights

In the town square, the lights do dance,
Glistening bright, they put you in trance.
Santa's on break, sipping hot cocoa,
While elves are all busy, putting on a show.

Mittens and hats, oh what a sight,
Snowflakes and giggles, pure delight.
Frosty's out stunting, he'll take a spin,
On skates made of ice, he's bound to win!

Laughter Trails Through Crisp Nights

Crisp air is filled with giggles and glee,
As snowmen debate who's the tallest, you see.
Some roast marshmallows, some just roast friends,
With stories that twist, but never quite end.

Sledding down hills, oh what a blast,
"Last one to base camp is too slow!" they gasp.
Hot chocolate spills, oh the sugary fun,
Each sip brings laughter, warmth for everyone.

A Symphony of Merry Melodies

Jingle bells ringing, off-key with flair,
Carolers stumble but they don't care.
Neighbors peek out with a curious frown,
As music unravels, all over the town.

Some sing like angels, some sound like goats,
A holiday choir, in wild, mismatched coats.
Each note a chuckle, each tune a grin,
As laughter spreads wide, let the festivities begin!

Holiday Wishes in Soft Snowfall

Snowflakes whisper sweetly, soft on the ground,
In a merry dance, they twirl all around.
Wishes are cast with each flake that lands,
For warmth, joy, and cookies baked by our hands.

Families gather, on blankets they huddle,
Picking the worst gifts, oh what a muddle!
With laughter like bells, shining bright in the air,
We treasure these moments, with fun everywhere.

Radiant Reflections

In the mirror, I see a face,
Wishing I'd grown some extra grace.
Hair's a mess, oh what a sight,
Maybe I'll just dim the light.

Brushed my teeth with a sock again,
Is it a trend? I can't pretend.
With toothpaste stains all over me,
I'm the Picasso of dentistry!

A Night of Delightful Whimsy

Oh, what a night for socks to dance,
They've taken on a strange romance.
The fridge hums, serenading a bee,
They're waltzing, just two left feet!

The cat decided to take a leap,
Right into the fishbowl—oh, what a heap!
Goldfish flew as if on parade,
Guess they're the stars of this charade!

Singing Through the Snow

With snowflakes falling, I made a ball,
Landed on my face—oh, that was a fall!
The snowman smiles, but he's got style,
His carrot nose? It makes me smile.

Singing loudly, a jolly tune,
The neighbors peek out—oh, they'll be marooned.
My dog joins in, howls quite off-key,
We're a winter concert, just wait and see!

Glimmers of Gratitude

Thankful for coffee that fuels my day,
Even if I spill it—hey, that's okay!
Grateful for friends who laugh at my jokes,
Especially the ones that tickle the folks.

Here's to the cookies that crumble and fall,
And the embarrassing stories I'll share with you all.
Each little moment, a spark that shines bright,
Life is a hoot, an endless delight!

Hearts United in Holiday Bliss

The turkey's dancing on the plate,
While grandpa's napping, isn't it great?
The pie's a mountain, oh what a sight,
Who knew that baking could start a fight?

The tree's on fire, or that's what they say,
Uncle Joe's sweater is truly a display.
The carols are loud, but off-key for sure,
As we all sing along, our laughter's the cure.

The gifts are wrapped with tape that's too strong,
We wrestle and tumble, it won't be long.
But when the paper flies like snow in the air,
We find out that socks are what we all share!

So here's to the chaos that holidays bring,
With cookies and chaos, let us all sing.
Hearts united, it's such a big mess,
May laughter and joy be our only stress!

Whispers of Good Cheer on Frosted Breath

The snowflakes fall with a tickle and twist,
While penguins slide by, can't help but insist:
They waddle with style on the ice all around,
While I try to stand, but I fall with a sound!

Hot cocoa's steaming, it's thick as a wall,
With marshmallows bobbing, they're having a ball.
But one little sip, and I soon lose my grace,
As the chocolate comes dancing all over my face!

The snowman I built takes on a new form,
With a carrot for a nose, he's the latest trendstorm.
He waves to the kids, but they giggle with glee,
When he leans a bit too close, "Is that a snow sneeze?"

So here's to the fun on this chilly good day,
With laughter and giggles, let worries decay.
With whispers of cheer tucked under each breath,
Let's spread the joy, it's the best kind of quest!

The Warmth of Familiar Faces

In the kitchen, pies are baked,
A cat on the counter, feeling great.
We laugh 'til we snort, it's a hoot,
While Uncle Joe's still stuck in his boot.

Old photos loom, those awkward years,
With hairdos so wild, we burst into tears.
A toast to the past, with clinks of glass,
To those funny moments that we let pass.

The food's all gone, but that's just fine,
We'll eat dessert and sip our wine.
Grandma's secret, it's worth the chase,
Her smile, the warmth of familiar face.

Feasting Under the Soft Glow

Table set, and legs a-swing,
Everyone's here for the tasty fling.
Dinner rolls buttered, on a strict diet,
Till Fred takes one and sets off a riot.

Beneath the glow of candles' dance,
We carve the turkey, but oh, what a chance!
Sister spills gravy all down her dress,
But we all just laugh, no need to stress.

As seconds are served, we can't help but gloat,
While Aunt Linda's soup almost made us choke.
Yet we binge on treats and laugh some more,
Life's too short, let's even the score!

Threads of Love Stitched Together

A quilt of memories laid out wide,
Each square tells tales, we giggle and bide.
Sewing mistakes that look quite neat,
Like grandma's attempts at knitting a sheet.

A patch of joy, a splash of flair,
Reminds us of days we barely could bear.
Socks mismatched, but love's thread binds,
In patterns of chaos, happiness finds.

Every stitch a chuckle, every knot a snare,
We patch up our hearts, with laughter to spare.
Those threads of love, colored so bright,
Warming our souls on the coldest of nights.

Beneath the Cloak of Snow

The snowflakes fall like a pillow fight,
We dash outside, what pure delight!
Snowmen rise with carrots for noses,
But our snowball war just plainly poses.

Hot cocoa waits, all marshmallowed,
But first, more snow! Our cheeks are crowded.
We trudge around, our boots get stuck,
Then slip and slide with squeals of luck.

The night's deep hush, a frosty glow,
As we gather 'round the fire's glow.
Beneath the cloak, all burdens shed,
Together we dream, while laughter's spread.

Gleeful Revelry in Candlelit Rooms

The candles flicker, shadows dance,
A questionable cake, all things askance.
We laugh at the table, spilled drinks and jokes,
Uncle Joe's slappery gets the best pokes.

A cat in a hat steals the spotlight,
While Aunt May's stories take off in flight.
With every bad pun, our laughter erupts,
And the night's silly antics are joyfully cupped.

As plates pile high, diets go on hold,
With cookies and cupcakes, a sweet scene unfolds.
We toast to mishaps, our bonds like glue,
In candlelit rooms, the merriment grew.

A Festival Where Spirits Soar

In the park, the balloons fill the sky,
A ferret in shorts, oh my, oh my!
With music so loud, it drowns out the noise,
As kids cannonball into puddles, what poise!

Cotton candy clouds, sticky and sweet,
While a juggler juggles his own two left feet.
We cheer for the clowns, in their oversized shoes,
Dancing like no one, with no fear of the blues.

There's face painting chaos, can you see the art?
A lion with wings? Now that's a fine start!
As laughter erupts in this colorful spree,
The festival thrives, and there's more fun to see.

The Bliss of Family Gatherings

Family dinners, where chaos is key,
Grandma's got smoke signals from the overcooked pea.
While cousins play tag, and my brother just trips,
We share secret glances through laughter and quips.

With a game of charades exploding in thrills,
Dad's miming a fish, yet we all get the chills.
And Aunt Sally's casserole needs its own plot,
We shove down our bites, declaring it hot!

With every 'remember when' shared with delight,
We build up our stories, oh what a sight!
Through giggles and jests, our hearts intertwine,
A blissful reunion, where love's the best wine.

Warmth in Every Shared Moment

Gather 'round the fire, let the tales ignite,
A funny game of who can sing right.
With marshmallows toasted to gooey perfection,
We all pause to savor this sweet connection.

The puppy runs wild, chasing shadows galore,
While Dad tries to leg lift the snack bowl once more.
In cozy old sweaters, we bubble with glee,
As we chat 'til we're sleepy, just you and me.

There's warmth in our laughter, a glow like the sun,
Every moment we share is a treasure begun.
With stories of mischief that never quite fail,
In warmth of togetherness, we happily sail.

Luminous Dreams on Frosted Air

In winter's chill, the snowflakes dance,
They twirl around in a happy prance.
A penguin slips on ice, what a sight!
But he just grins, thinks it's pure delight.

The stars above wear frosty crowns,
While snowmen sport their carrot frowns.
Each breath we take, a cloud unfurls,
In dreams where laughter's the precious pearl.

The Magic of Sweet Reunions

Oh, friends returning, it's quite the show,
With hugs that twirl, and laughter's glow.
We feast on cookies, talk about life,
While dodging the question of who's got a wife.

One brings a cat, another a dog,
They argue over who's the bigger hog.
Amidst the chaos, there's joy so sweet,
With stories that dance on our happy feet.

Bright Eyes and Warm Hugs

Bright eyes sparkling like morning dew,
Warm hugs that make a chilly day new.
A puppy jumps in, with tail all a-wag,
And suddenly, everyone's wearing a rag.

We play a game called "Who can fall?"
Laughter erupts with a bouncy ball.
A tickle fight brews in the sunny land,
And all of us giggle, it's perfectly planned.

Whispers of Goodwill in the Night

At twilight's call, we gather 'round,
With secrets shared in a joyous sound.
A ghost tells jokes, but they're rather tame,
And we all agree, he's earned some fame.

The moon's our light, with its silver grin,
As we roast marshmallows and sip our gin.
The final whisper as we say goodnight,
Is all about dreams that shine ever bright.

Dreams and Wishes Intertwined

In a land where cats can fly,
And fish can play the lute,
I dream of pies that never end,
And shoes that dance with boots.

Wishes ride on unicorns,
Through rainbows made of cheese,
I toss my dreams into the stars,
And hope for some more peas.

Giraffes wear hats and sunglasses,
While lions sip sweet tea,
I wish for more of this delight,
And for my dog, to speak with glee.

The Lantern of Togetherness

We gather 'round the glowing light,
With snacks that jingle too,
Sharing tales of silly fumbles,
Like tripping on a shoe.

The lantern swings with gentle ease,
While laughter fills the air,
A toast to friends who make us smile,
In moments that we share.

With marshmallows on our fingers,
And chocolate on our cheek,
Together we can conquer all,
Even the toughest week.

A Celebration of Life's Little Joys

Ice cream drips on sunny days,
And socks that don't quite match,
The thrill of finding lost TV remotes,
Oh what a perfect catch!

The joy of sprouting belly laughs,
And cookies warm and bright,
Jumping in the puddles,
A splash that feels just right.

Moments spent in silly games,
Like racing funny bikes,
Let's cherish every little thing,
For joy is what life spikes!

Luminous Love in the Winter's Embrace

When snowflakes dance like happy cues,
And mittens start to clash,
We bundle close to share the warmth,
And not get cold and brash.

The cocoa spills with marshmallow dreams,
As laughter fills the night,
In every hug, there's warmth enough,
To melt away each fright.

In winter's chill, our hearts aglow,
With love that shines so bright,
We twirl with joy, in frosty air,
Together, what a sight!

Magical Tides of Holiday Spirit

The cookies vanished in a blink,
The reindeer drank the milk, I think!
Wrapped gifts are hiding in plain sight,
I swear that elf just took a flight!

The snowman's belly, round and wide,
Might roll away on winter's ride!
Gifts with ribbons all tied in knots,
Oh look! There go the dancing pots!

A tree adorned with tinsel bright,
And lights that flicker through the night.
But where's the cat? Under the tree?
Knocking baubles, oh what glee!

So here's to all the silly fun,
From baking treats to setting sun!
Holiday cheer, a crazy ride,
The magic's here, just take your stride!

The Glow of Comforting Presence

A cozy chair, a warm embrace,
With socks that match, oh what a grace!
The blanket soft, it hugs me tight,
It whispers, 'Stay, we'll be alright.'

The cocoa's steaming, marshmallows float,
While movies play, I'll just emote.
Laughter spills like happy rain,
When friends drop by to share the gain!

With every sip, the world is bright,
A glow of joy, a pure delight.
In fuzzy slippers, we all unite,
A gathering that feels just right!

So here's to warmth, to love's sweet glow,
With every moment, let fondness grow.
In this bright hug, let's dance and sing,
For in each heart, the joy we bring!

Tracing Paths of Cheerful Memories

We stroll through parks, paths made of gold,
With stories shared, our hearts unfold.
From childhood games to secrets lost,
Together we laugh, no matter the cost.

A ride on swings, we reach for the sky,
Like flying fish, soaring up high!
The tickle fights and silly jokes,
Are cherished tales, our hearts invoke!

With snapshots taken, smiles on our face,
In every moment, we find our place.
Through ups and downs, we walked as one,
Our memories bind us, never undone!

So here's to paths we trod with glee,
Each twist and turn, our jubilee.
In every laugh, in every cheer,
Together we shine, year after year!

A Gallery of Grateful Hearts

In frames of joy, our laughs, our plays,
A mix of colors, brightening days!
Grateful hearts in every smile,
We cherish moments, mile by mile.

From simple things, like hugs so tight,
To dancing under the moonlight!
With friends who cheer, and family dear,
These memories sparkle, oh so clear!

The tales we tell, oh what a ride,
With gratitude, we're side by side.
In every snapshot, a loving art,
A gallery built from each kind heart!

So let us dance, and let us sing,
For grateful hearts, joy's everything.
In every frame, our spirits soar,
In love we gather, forevermore!

Cocoa and Carols

A steaming mug, oh what a treat,
With marshmallows just can't be beat.
Sipping slow, a cozy cheer,
While off-key voices ring in my ear.

Snowflakes dance, the wind does howl,
Outside the window, I see the owl.
In a sweater two sizes too wide,
I'm ready for holiday joy to collide!

A Tapestry of Tidings

With cookies made by questionable hands,
And fruitcake born from far-off lands.
My aunt's dessert, a wobbly mess,
Yet we praise her skills, oh what a stress!

Tinsel tangled in the tree,
Just one more strand, can't you see?
A cat now swings, in pure delight,
Knocking baubles left and right!

The Night of Glistening Wishes

Stars above in a twinkling row,
What did I want? I don't quite know.
A gift to wrap that won't fall flat,
Or just a holiday nap on the mat?

When midnight strikes, we all do shout,
Then spill our secrets, there's no doubt.
With cookies gone, now crumbs abound,
Our wishes lost, but laughter found!

Spheres of Light and Laughter

Orbs of color on branches sway,
They twinkle bright, come out to play.
The dog's confused, he thinks it's food,
A festive chase, now that's our mood!

Neighbors' lights, a blinding show,
Who won the contest? No one knows.
We judge them all, with cookies in hand,
And dance around in winter's land!

Celebrations in a Winter Wonderland

Snowflakes dance like tiny elves,
Frosty beards on snowman selves.
Sledding down the hill with glee,
Hot cocoa spills on me, oh me!

Jingle bells are out of tune,
Reindeer munching on a prune.
Carols sung off-key for fun,
Santa's lost his way, oh run!

Giant stockings, all too wide,
Filled with toys we cannot hide.
Mittens lost on every hand,
Winter games, it's snowman land!

Family feasts with food galore,
Leftovers spilling from the door.
Candles lit that smell like pie,
"Who ate my cake?" a woeful cry!

Hearts Aglow with Festive Cheer

Twinkling lights on every street,
Home-baked cookies, hard to beat.
Gifts wrapped poorly, what a sight,
Grandma's sweater, oh so bright!

Laughter fills the chilly air,
A cat's in the tree, who would dare?
Muffin tops that rise so high,
Fruitcake that could make you cry!

Mistletoe hangs, a sneak attack,
Someone spills, they can't go back.
Snowball fights that lead to tears,
But hugs and joy drown out the fears.

Jolly faces, rosy red,
Gossip about who's well-fed.
With each cheer, our spirits soar,
Until next year, who could want more?

The Joy of Giving and Receiving

Wrappings ripped and laughter loud,
Granny's gift, oh what a crowd!
Socks and ties, the usual bore,
But candy canes? Everyone's chore!

Gift cards galore, what a thrill,
Yet every year, same old drill.
A sweater two sizes too small,
"Just wear it!" they all call!

Surprises wrapped with love and flair,
A puzzle missing pieces, beware!
Ribbons tangled, such a mess,
Trading gifts, who's the best guess?

Cheerful hearts, we all unite,
Minty treats for pure delight.
With every hug and friendly grin,
The joy of giving's where we win!

Frosty Air and Kindred Souls

Bundled up in hats and coats,
Hot soup served that's sure to gloat.
Snowflakes land upon our nose,
Wishing for a snowball rose!

Winter games and chilly hands,
Sledding down the snowy lands.
Hot cider's steaming in our cups,
But first, let's swap our winter pups!

Fireside tales and spooky fright,
Candy left out late at night.
Friends who share their frosty breath,
Tell me, is snowball fight 'til death?

As stars twinkle in the night,
We wrap our friendship, oh so tight.
Laughter echoes through the trees,
Winter's warmth brings hearts to ease!

Enchanted Revelry

In a forest of glitter, the fairies did prance,
They lost all their shoes in a wild, silly dance.
With toads in top hats and frogs in a tie,
They sang out of tune—oh my, how they'd fly!

A gnome by the stream tried to juggle some fish,
But they all just flopped—what a soggy wish!
The pixies were laughing, they danced in delight,
As the moon turned to cheese, what a magical sight!

A wizard tripped over his own brand-new broom,
While casting a spell that went boom, boom, boom!
But instead of a potion, he brewed up some cheer,
And the forest erupted in raucous good cheer!

So if you find magic, just know it's a show,
With laughter and giggles, let your worries go!
Grab a gnome, do a jig, let the funny times flow,
It's all just enchanted, and that's how we roll!

Tinsel Trails

On a shiny, bright path where the tinsel does twinkle,
Elves gather round with some gooey sweet krinkle.
They wrap up a cat in a garland so fine,
But the cat simply stretched, claimed the tinsel as mine!

An otter once sliding by snagged a red ball,
And tripped on a cookie that caused quite a fall.
The reindeer rolled over, all wrapped up in bows,
While the snowmen debated their carrot-y noses!

A parrot squawked loudly, "Where's my shiny hat?"
And a squirrel in mittens said, "You look like a brat!"
But laughter erupted, with giggles galore,
As everyone cheered, "Let's party some more!"

So if you see tinsel, just follow along,
Where the laughter is hearty and nothing feels wrong!
For in the world of the wacky and bright,
Tinsel trails always lead to pure, silly delight!

Melody of the Firelight

By the crackling fire, the marshmallows dance,
S'mores in hand, we all join in the chance.
A raccoon on a log plays the drums with great flair,
While fireflies flicker, like stars in the air!

Someone's sweet grandma starts singing off-key,
Her cat joins the chorus, what fun it can be!
With laughter and cheers, we pass round the pie,
And the raccoon just nods, a wise pop star nearby!

In the glow of the embers, the stories unfold,
Of a dragon who danced with a knight brave and bold.
But the knight tripped on twigs and fell flat on his face,
While the dragon just giggled—oh, what a disgrace!

So gather around as the melodies play,
With marshmallows roasting, it's a fun-filled array!
In the heartbeat of firelight, let joy be the spark,
Creating sweet memories 'til well after dark!

Crystalline Moments

A snowflake fell down, with a twirl and a spin,
It landed on a nose, causing giggles to begin.
With ice skating penguins who slipped on the lake,
They crash into snowmen, what a marvelous shake!

A walrus in shades rides a sleigh made of ice,
While seals throw snowballs—oh, how they entice!
With laughter cascading like icicles bright,
Each moment's a treasure, a shimmering sight!

In a world made of glimmer, it's hard not to grin,
As polar bears dance in a sparkly spin.
They strut with such style, each paw so refined,
Making crystalline memories one of a kind!

So remember the laughter when winter is here,
With moments like these, let's spread lots of cheer!
For in the chill of the season, let joy take its flight,
And dance with the snowflakes, from morning to night!

Frosty Fingerprints of Delight

Snowflakes fall, a chilly spree,
I caught one on my tongue, whee!
Frosty prints across my nose,
Coughing up the snowman's toes.

Sledding down the hill so fast,
I crashed and made a snow fort cast.
Hot cocoa spills, a marshmallow war,
"Who left the door open?" I implore!

Penguins slide in winter's game,
Trying to win an ice-cube fame.
Snowball fights with friends galore,
I'll still deny, I started that score!

Frosty nights and sparks that fly,
Chasing dreams beneath the sky.
Giggles echo through the trees,
Winter's magic brings such glee!

Hearthside Happenings

Crackling fire and cozy chairs,
Grandma's tales and silly glares.
Hot pies cooling on the sill,
"Don't eat them all!" I get my fill.

Uncle Bob tries to dance a jig,
Tripping over the coffee gig.
Cat jumps high, then lands a flop,
While Grandpa snoozes, not a hop.

We tell ghost stories, all aglow,
While the wind outside starts to blow.
Lights strung up, a festive sight,
"Who's eating all the cookies tonight?"

Mistletoe hangs above our heads,
Kisses fly like rumors spread.
Joyful laughter fills the space,
With love that's warming every face!

Embracing the Seasonal Spirit

Leaves are turning, colors bright,
Fall is here, oh what a sight!
Pumpkin spice and sweater snug,
Watch out for that sneaky bug!

Cider sips on chilly days,
Finding corn mazes in a haze.
Scarecrows dance, but I can't tell,
Which one's real? They do so well!

Bonfire nights with friends so dear,
Roasting marshmallows, full of cheer.
S'mores so sticky, we need a plan,
While squirrels plot their winter span.

The leaves descend, it's nature's art,
Let's jump in piles; it's the best part!
Embracing fall, with giggles loud,
Cuz every moment feels so proud!

Lullabies of Light

Stars above twinkle in delight,
Whispering secrets in the night.
Candles glow, casting soft beams,
As I drift off into dreams.

Flickering flames dance a waltz,
"Is that a noise or just my fault?"
Teddy bear holds me tight and close,
In a world of wonder, he's the most.

Moonbeams shine through the window pane,
Chasing away the worries, plain.
Crickets hum a lullaby sweet,
While shadows softly tap their feet.

So close your eyes, feel the air,
Dream of places without a care.
Lullabies of light tonight,
In slumber's arms, all feels right!

Whispers of Merriment

In the kitchen, cookies pop,
A cat does a wild flip-flop.
Flour dust and giggles blend,
Baking fun that has no end.

Uncle Fred's joke falls flat,
A parrot screams, 'You're such a brat!'
Grandma's knitting knits a meme,
'Twas the night of the failed cream.'

Sprinkles dance upon the cake,
A voice yells, 'What's that noise? A quake!'
Pumpkin pie takes a wild dive,
And now we've lost the driver hive.

With laughter echoing all around,
The essence of joy can be found.
So raise a glass, let spirits soar,
In the land of fun, we all want more.

Starlit Embrace

Underneath the moon so bright,
We lost our way—oh, what a sight!
A raccoon stole my sandwich dear,
Now I'm left with just my beer!

Neighbors dancing, what a scene,
Clad in costumes—think Halloween!
A chicken leads a conga line,
I swear that rooster drank some wine.

Stars above join in the spree,
A shooting star falls, near me!
But wait, I see it's just a kite,
The kids flew up, what a delight!

In the starlit night, we prance,
Under twinkling lights, we dance.
Embracing joy with giggles loud,
Together, we form a silly crowd.

The Glow of Giving

Wrapped presents with bows askew,
Who's stealing cookies? I think it's you!
Lights are flashing, red and green,
The ugliest sweater you've ever seen.

A gift that giggles when you shake,
What could it be? A giant cake?
Mom bursts out with a cheer and grin,
'You know I'm on a diet, right? Win!'

While Santa's stuck on the roof,
His sleigh now plays a funny spoof.
"My reindeer need a break, oh dear!"
Guess we'll walk, it's all sincere.

In the glow of laughter bright,
We find the joy in every bite.
So gather round, let's share the cheer,
For the glow of giving is finally here!

Laughter Beneath the Mistletoe

Caught beneath the mistletoe,
A chance to laugh, oh don't be slow!
A bad dance move leads to a trip,
And down we go—a comedic flip!

Friendship's woes, romantic fumbles,
Kisses stolen, laughter tumbles.
The dog jumps in, a curious guest,
And all our hearts are now at rest.

Hot cocoa spills across the floor,
Marshmallows bounce, who could want more?
So raise your cup, let's clink and cheer,
With laughter beneath, we draw near.

Through silly slips and joyful sighs,
We share sweet moments, no surprise.
The magic grows, in hugs we find,
Love and laughter, forever intertwined.

Festive Echoes of Laughter

The turkey's gone, the pie was great,
We laugh at uncle's dance, oh wait!
With tinsel tangled in the tree,
We sip our cocoa, full of glee.

The cat's in the lights, a glittering sight,
Chasing shadows in the night.
Grandma's sweater makes us cringe,
But we still let her take the fringe!

The kids are running, full of cheer,
While parents moan, 'Holiday beer!'
We toast the joys, the silly fights,
As laughter echoes through the nights.

So raise your glass, let's celebrate,
With jokes and stories we narrate.
In festive spirit, we unite,
With echoes of laughter, pure delight.

Twinkling Moments of Togetherness

The lights are bright, the mood is right,
Family gathered, such delight.
Cookies stacked, a sweet display,
We munch and laugh the night away.

Grandpa's snoring's like a bell,
While kids play tag, oh can't you tell?
Each twinkling moment warms the heart,
In this big, crazy family art.

A toast to love, a cheer for fun,
In mismatched socks we laugh and run.
The memories made, so sweet and bold,
In this cozy chaos, joy unfolds.

So grab a sibling, spin around,
Our twinkling moments know no bounds.
Together here, we share a grin,
In the warmth of love, our hearts will win.

The Dance of Shimmering Ornaments

The ornaments shine, they spin and sway,
A little too close, they're on display.
With every jingle, a secret told,
Of holiday mischief from days of old.

The kittens pounce, the dog's on guard,
As angels look on, it's a little bizarre.
We laugh at the chaos, the glittering mess,
This dance of ornaments, we confess!

Grandma's tales of Christmas past,
With every step, we're having a blast.
In mismatched pairs, we take a spin,
In this holiday magic, where do we begin?

So swirl and twirl 'neath the golden light,
Our hearts are aglow, everything's right.
With shimmering decorations all around,
In this festive dance, joy is found.

Songs of Cheer Beneath the Evergreen

Beneath the tree, we sing so loud,
With every note, we feel so proud.
Grandpa's off-key, but we don't care,
In this joyful moment, love fills the air.

The kids are giggling, trying to keep,
A straight face while Grandma's asleep.
With jingles and laughter, our hearts take flight,
In the warmth of the evening, everything's bright.

As carols play, the cookies disappear,
We're caught in giggles, can't hold back cheer.
In this symphony of joy we weave,
Beneath the evergreen, we truly believe.

So raise your voice, let the songs resound,
With every cheer, our love is profound.
In this magical time, let's all convene,
With songs of cheer beneath the evergreen.

Crystals of Joy in the Winter Air

Frosty flakes dance all around,
As I fall face-first on the ground.
Laughter echoes through the trees,
Winter's gift is just a sneeze.

Bundled up like a snowman stout,
Hot cocoa spills, oh what a clout!
Snowball fights in a joyful blur,
Who knew winter could make us purr?

Shoveling paths and laughing wide,
My dog takes off, I just can't hide!
Chasing him down, slipping in snow,
This winter fun is quite the show.

In the chill, we find our glow,
Crystals of joy, oh how they flow!
With each icy breath, we share our glee,
Winter's a laugh, just wait and see!

Sledding Through Fields of Delight

Off we go with shouts and cheers,
Sleds in tow, ignoring our fears.
At the top, the world looks grand,
Then we tumble, oh, who's got land?

Down we slide, a thrilling race,
Landing flat, oh what a face!
Snow flies high, boots filled with white,
Sledding's fun, especially at night.

Laughter rings in the frosty air,
Who knew sleds could be a dare?
With winter's chill, our hearts are bright,
Chasing delight in pure moonlight.

When the day ends with winter's mist,
We hope this joy can't be dismissed.
Every bump and giggle we've shared,
Is a memory of fun we've all bared.

Banding Together in Holiday Cheer

Gather 'round, it's time to feast,
Turkey's here, we'll munch at least!
Gravy splatters, oh what a sight,
Grandma's dance? A pure delight!

Decorations hung a bit crooked,
Guess the strings need more of a look,
Lights are tangled, but spirits soar,
Nothing beats laughter, who could ask for more?

Cookies stacked and pies galore,
Uncle Bob's jokes? We dread the roar!
Yet in this chaos, joy is found,
Hugs and cheers keep love profound.

As we band together, hearts entwined,
Holiday cheer, so well-defined.
In every laugh, we hold so dear,
These funny mishaps bring us cheer!

A Cornucopia of Warmth and Kindness

In a kettle sits a soup divine,
With every ladle, good vibes align.
Friends drawn close 'round the fire's glow,
Spreading warmth, as we come and go.

With every hug and shared delight,
A kindness spark ignites the night.
Hot drinks flow, and stories are spun,
Laughter echoes, our hearts are one.

The potluck spread is quite the sight,
Dishes piled up, a true delight!
Granny's casserole, the star of the show,
But I'll stick to cookies, just so you know.

In this cornucopia of goodwill,
Every moment gives a happy thrill.
With warmth and kindness, we share the cheer,
This feast of laughter brings us near.

Frosty Wishes and Warmth

When snowflakes dance and fall so white,
I bundle up, what a frosty sight!
Hot cocoa spills, oh what a mess,
I taste it twice, I must confess.

Chilly noses, cheeks aglow,
Build a snowman, head to toe!
His carrot nose, a little crude,
Yet somehow, he still looks shrewd.

Scarves wrapped tight, I waddle along,
Dancing feet to winter's song.
But oh, the ice, it takes my feet,
A slip, a slide, my icy treat!

Frosty wishes fill the air,
More hot chocolate, if you dare!
With laughter loud, our spirits soar,
Let's wish for snow, and then some more.

Tidings Wrapped in Glee

Here come the tidings, wrapped so tight,
A gift of giggles, pure delight!
With paper ripped, the chaos grows,
Surprise! It's socks, as everyone knows.

Bells are jingling, cheer abounds,
But who can find the lost dog's hound?
Under the tree, he takes a nap,
As we all fight for the last gift wrap.

Cookies baked with love and flair,
Oops, they vanished—in thin air!
With crumbs that trace a path so clear,
We know our little thief is near.

With laughter echoing, hearts so light,
The magic of warmth fills the night.
Tidings wrapped in silly cheer,
Give me some cake, we'll persevere!

Kindred Spirits by the Hearth

By the hearth, we gather round,
With jokes and stories—fun abound!
Cushions tossed and laughter loud,
In our cozy little crowd.

Sipping tea, we share a grin,
A game of charades, let's begin!
I act a frog, they scream and shout,
But what's my name? I'm lost, no doubt!

Footlights dim, the drama flows,
In our hearts, the friendship grows.
With marshmallows toasted just right,
We tell our tales deep into night.

Kindred spirits, we unite,
With jokes and laughter, pure delight.
In this cozy space, hearts are bright,
By the hearth, all feels just right!

A Tapestry of Shared Smiles

In a world of colors, bold and bright,
We weave our tales, with joy and light.
Each thread a memory, spun with glee,
A tapestry of you and me.

With every laugh, our bond does grow,
Inside jokes that only we know.
We trip on words, and tumble too,
Yet through it all, we laugh anew.

Picnics shared under blue skies,
With sandwiches that somehow surprise!
Did you pack this? It's made of foam!
However it tastes, it feels like home.

A shared smile brightens any day,
In this tapestry, we'll laugh and play.
So here's to us—friends true and wise,
With shared memories, our spirits rise!

Sweet Surrender to Festive Joy

When holiday lights start to twinkle bright,
I discover my diet takes a flight.
With cookies in hand and pie in my lap,
I surrender to joy, no thoughts of the gap.

The eggnog is flowing, the cheer is profound,
I dance like a turkey that just gained some ground.
Wrapped up in laughter, my fingers are sticky,
These festive delights make my heart feel so picky.

As carols are sung, I join in the fun,
While munching on treats, I say, "Just one more, hon!"
In sweaters so bright, I twirl and I sway,
With crumbs on my chin, who cares anyway?

So raise up your glasses, let's toast to the year,
With merriment flowing and holiday cheer.
Life's sweetest surrender is found in each bite,
When festive joy calls, it feels oh so right!

The Magic of Shared Memories

Remember that time we lost all the maps?
We circled the block, oh how we had laps!
In search of a diner, or maybe a brew,
Every turn led us to a different view.

And how could we forget that lasagna fight?
With noodles and sauce, oh what a delight!
We laughed and we slurped till our bellies were round,
Those moments of chaos, the best to be found.

Each memory forged like a mystical spell,
Crafted through laughter, we wear it so well.
From mishaps of travel to pie in the face,
We cherish these stories, our own little space.

So here's to the laughs and the joy we have made,
Each shared memory like sunshine that stayed.
In the book of our lives, it's the funniest part,
The magic of friendship that's close to the heart!

Kind Hearts Under Star-Filled Skies

Under the stars, we gather tonight,
With laughter and joy, everything feels right.
Each story shared sparkles like stars,
Our hearts are so kind, they'll travel so far.

The moon shines a light on our silly jokes,
We dance like the owls, just a bunch of blokes.
In comfy old sweaters, we share and we cheer,
With s'mores and hot cocoa, we hold them near.

As campfire flames flicker and sway,
We reminisce 'bout life in the silliest way.
From cringy old moments to plans yet unseen,
Down memory lane, we happily glean.

So raise up your voice, my dear friends, don't be shy,
Under star-filled skies, our spirits can fly.
In kindness, we find that true friendship ignites,
Making stars twinkle brighter on these wondrous nights!

Glimmers of Hope and Merriment

As winter winds blow and the snow starts to fall,
We gather together, let's have a great ball!
With laughter as sparkles, and joy as our guide,
Glimmers of hope are found deep inside.

The jingle bells ring, how our spirits they lift,
We share silly stories, each one a small gift.
From walls covered in tinsel to lights all aglow,
Merriment dances, it puts on a show.

Let's bake us some cookies, a recipe wild,
With sprinkles and icing, oh aren't we beguiled?
With each little bite, our hearts start to sing,
Glimmers of hope are our favorite thing!

So for all of the moments that bring us delight,
Let's cheer for our friendships, our personal light.
In the chill of the season, let warmth take its stance,
Glimmers of hope give us all a great chance!

An Evening of Serendipity

A cat in a hat, oh what a sight,
Twirled on the carpet, almost took flight.
The dog chased the mouse, with great delight,
While the goldfish rolled its eyes, not quite right.

Dinner was served, a pie made of peas,
I wanted dessert, but oh, what a tease!
The chef was a squirrel, cooking with ease,
And he danced on the counter, shouting, "More cheese!"

We laughed at the chaos, with friends by our side,
Each silly mishap, a hilarious ride.
The laughter kept growing, our hearts opened wide,
In this evening of joy, we all let love abide.

As moonlight adorned the delightful scene,
We forged silly memories, like never seen.
With snacks made of candy, our faces were keen,
In moments like these, life is surely serene.

Love's Evergreen Glow

In a garden of socks, where strange things grow,
A pair of mismatched ones stole the show.
They tangoed and twirled in a soft, gentle flow,
And the viewers all cheered, 'What a delightful show!'

Then came a shy mitten, snug on a hand,
That whispered sweet nothings, pretending it's grand.
With fingers entwined, they both took a stand,
And twinkled like stars in a magical land.

The trees all jiggled, the breeze let it flow,
As love bloomed around, in its vibrant glow.
The sun cast a wink, from above so low,
Saying, 'Love's evergreen, just let it grow!'

So here's to the quirky, the funny, the bright,
In each silly moment, we find pure delight.
With laughter as glue, our hearts take flight,
In love's evergreen glow, everything feels right.

Radiant Fireside Whispers

By the fireside, we sat with a snack,
A marshmallow mishap—it fell with a clack!
It wobbled and jiggled, no way to hold back,
And the dog caught it quick, just like a full sack!

Our stories danced like the flames' warm embrace,
Of failed cooking, mishaps, and a funny face.
The laughter erupted, we found our own space,
In this radiant moment, we were filled with grace.

With s'mores on the side, and hot cocoa to sip,
We toasted to friendship, let no detail slip.
Each giggle and grin took us on a trip,
In the fireside's glow, we relaxed with a dip.

So gather your friends, let the warmth start to spin,
With jokes that will make your own cheeks wear thin.
In fireside whispers, where laughter begins,
Create cherished moments, together we win.

Starlit Laughter and Candlelight

Under the stars, we gathered so tight,
With candlelight flickers, our spirits took flight.
The fireflies joined in, a whimsical sight,
As we danced in the glow, what pure delight!

One tripped on a shoelace, fell into a chair,
The laughter erupted, we couldn't help stare.
With jokes flying high, like balloons in the air,
We rolled on the grass, without a single care.

The moon winked at us, joining our cheer,
As stories were shared, the smart and the queer.
With giggles and snorts, we forgot every fear,
Creating a memory that all would revere.

So here's to the laughter, in moments like these,
With starlit connections, we do as we please.
In candlelight warmth, let all hearts be at ease,
For laughter and love are the sweetest of keys.

Radiance of Togetherness

In a world of chirpy chaos, we share a laugh,
While socks go missing, and pets steal the path.
Our kitchen's a battle, but we're chefs supreme,
With burnt toast and smoke, we still chase our dream.

We dance like no one's watching, except that one cat,
Who judges our moves while she lounges flat.
A sock puppet show, starring a broom,
Reveals our true talent—living in a room!

Picture us laughing, with pasta as hair,
Creating bizarre art, without a single care.
Our friendship's a circus, a comedy club,
We're the stars of the show, give us a scrub!

So here's to the chaos, the joy and delight,
Through spills and odd moments, we shine ever bright.
Together we giggle, through thick and through thin,
In the carnival of life, we'll always win!

Evergreens and Heartfelt Greetings

In the forest of pine, we shout a warm cheer,
To trees that are taller, and squirrels that jeer.
We hang up our socks on the evergreen tree,
Hoping Santa won't mind our quirky esprit.

With snowflakes a-falling, we build a fine guy,
A snowman who's wearing a turtleneck tie.
He waves as we giggle, adorned with a smile,
Just don't let him melt—it'll take a short while!

We sip on hot cocoa, with marshmallows galore,
Each sip brings us giggles, who could ask for more?
Our festive spirits soar, as we sing loud and clear,
With the echoes of laughter, can't help but endear!

Evergreens whisper our secrets in glee,
While we dance in the snow, just you and me.
With heartfelt greetings wrapped tight in a bow,
We cherish the warmth in the cold, don't you know?

Sipping Cocoa Under Starry Skies

With mugs full of cocoa, we sit hand in hand,
Under a blanket of stars, a soft, cozy land.
The moon gives us winks, like it knows our plan,
To spill all the secrets that linger, oh man!

With marshmallows floating, the cocoa turns sweet,
A concoction so dreamy, it's hard to beat.
We share our wild dreams, from Mars to the moon,
While the crickets serenade our silly tunes.

Tickling our noses, the chilly wind blows,
But laughter ignites, and our friendship just glows.
In the warmth of the moment, we forget all our woes,
As stars twinkle softly, the magic just grows.

So here's to the nights of sweet cocoa sips,
To the stitches of laughter and warm tongue-tips.
Under the canvas of dark, with hearts ever wise,
We sip cocoa together, beneath starry skies!

Love's Embrace in the Snow

In the snowy embrace, we tumble and roll,
With laughter like music, straight from the soul.
Our noses turn red, our cheeks rosy too,
As we build a snow fort, just me and you.

With snowflakes in hair, we dance hand in hand,
The world turns to magic, like a shimmering land.
Each twirl is a giggle, each fall is a cheer,
In this winter wonderland, our hearts feel so near.

The cocoa is calling, with whipped cream on top,
As we chat about snowmen and never plan to stop.
The warmth of your smile is my ultimate bliss,
Even in frosty moments, it's you that I miss.

So let's paint the town with love all aglow,
In the frosty embrace, where the chilly winds blow.
Together we'll conquer the white winter show,
In love's soft embrace, let the snowflakes just flow!

Merriment in Every Sparkling Gaze

In a world where socks don't match,
We laugh and dance, no need to hatch.
The silly hats atop our heads,
Turn ordinary days to joy-filled threads.

With every bite of cake so sweet,
We twirl like whirlwinds on our feet.
A splash of drink, a wink, a tease,
Life's too short, so laugh with ease.

We prance like goats in a field of hay,
And chase our worries far away.
Each sparkling gaze, a spark so bright,
Fills every moment with pure delight.

In this circus life we roam,
With giggles echoing like a poem.
Merriment gleams in every eye,
In this joyful dance, we learn to fly.

The Lasting Glow of Togetherness

Gathered round with friends so dear,
We swap our tales, we share a cheer.
With chips and dip upon our lap,
We fit together like a cozy nap.

The lasting glow of laughter bright,
Chasing away the dark of night.
Our mishaps make the best of shows,
Like tripping over garden hose.

With every smile, another snack,
We're tight-knit folks, and that's a fact.
Through thick and thin, we hold on tight,
Together we shine, purest light.

As years roll by, we'll still engage,
In this wild dance, we turn the page.
The lasting glow, forever stays,
In hearts and minds, it brightly plays.

Gladsome Smiles in Festive Harmony

With garlands hung and cookies baked,
We gather 'round, no plans are faked.
Each gladsome smile, a sight to see,
In this wild world, it's you and me.

We sing off-key, the notes collide,
But in our hearts, the joy won't hide.
With silly jokes and jolly cheer,
We toast to fun, our spirits clear.

The jingle bells ring loud and bright,
We dance beneath the twinkling light.
With cheers that echo, laughter blooms,
We fill this place with joy that zooms.

In festive harmony we sway,
Making memories that come to play.
A gladsome smile, a moment sweet,
Life's a feast, let's eat and greet.

A Night where Spirits Sing

As the stars twinkle in the sky,
We gather 'round, the spirits fly.
With joyful hearts, we start to swing,
Under the moon, our laughter rings.

Each clink of glasses brings a cheer,
A toast to friends we hold so dear.
With tales of yore that make us grin,
We spin our yarns, let the night begin.

The music plays, we lose our cares,
Dancing wildly, tossing hair.
With every spin, we dip and sway,
In this grand night, we find our way.

A night of joy, where spirits sing,
In every heart, a little spring.
We'll laugh and dance till break of dawn,
For in this night, we all belong.

The Spirit of Giving's Embrace

In a world full of queues and long lines,
A gift from the heart is where love shines.
Unwrap my socks, oh what a surprise,
They've got more holes than my best alibis!

With cookies to share, they crumble and break,
Even Santa might frown at this big mistake.
But laughter abounds, it's all in good cheer,
What matters is love, whether cozy or sheer.

Mirth in the Winter's Chill

Snowflakes are falling; my nose is red,
I thought I'd go sledding, but fell on my head.
Frosty the snowman just waved and then ran,
I should've stayed indoors, but I'm not a smart man!

Hot cocoa spills while I dance in delight,
My marshmallows swim—we'll need a lifeboat tonight.
The winter may chill, but laughter's the key,
Let's warm up our hearts with some cocoa and glee!

A Night of Merry Encounters

At the party, they gathered, all dressed up tight,
Some wore reindeer antlers, what a funny sight!
I stepped on the cat while I tried to impress,
And tripped on the tinsel—oh, what a mess!

We danced to the tunes of the holiday cheer,
But someone brought fruitcake—a real nightmare here.
So we laughed and we played, in this odd celebration,
What's better than friends to spark jubilation?

Glowing Faces Beneath the Mistletoe

Beneath the mistletoe, a sweet little spot,
I stood with my crush, but forgot what I'd thought.
With a wink and a grin, my heart started racing,
Then I turned to the side—oh no, I was spacing!

Instead of a kiss, I got a big hug,
With mistletoe drooping, still cozy and snug.
We both laughed it off, our cheeks all aglow,
Who needs a romance? Friends are the real show!

The Gift of Togetherness

We gathered 'round the table wide,
With Uncle Joe and his dog by side.
A feast of joy and laughter loud,
And Auntie Sue in her Christmas shroud.

The kids are bouncing, scream and shout,
While Gramps is trying to figure out.
What's a TikTok? What's the fuss?
It's just a cat that rides a bus!

We dance in circles, trip and fall,
While grandmas play their Christmas brawl.
The pie is gone, oh what a scene,
Now we must blame the family bean!

Togetherness means love's delight,
And foolishness that feels just right.
So here's to cheer and hearty laughs,
In every hug and silly gaffs.

Frosted Feasts

We've baked some cookies, oh what fun,
But now they look like we just run.
With sprinkles stuck to frosted ears,
And frosting rivers, oh dear, oh dear!

The cake is leaning, a sad display,
Like my cousin's hair on New Year's Day.
We planned a roast that's golden brown,
Yet managed to burn a nook in town!

The roast is dancing, ready to flee,
As grandma yells, "Don't munch on me!"
With gingerbread men that just won't stand,
We wonder how they became so bland.

But laughter fills the holiday air,
With family squabbling everywhere.
If food's a mess, we cheer and toast,
For frosted feasts we love the most!

Candles and Comfort

Candles flicker, shadows play,
While Gramps recounts his quirkiest day.
Mom's knitted socks, so bright and bold,
Have holes that make us feel quite cold.

We sip hot cocoa, marshmallows dive,
While dad warms up like twenty-five.
He tells the tale of his funny sweater,
With reindeer dancing, oh, what a debtor!

The glow of lights, like fireflies,
While Aunt May wears her Christmas pies.
We play charades and mock the night,
As candles melt and spirits light.

Comfort's there with every laugh,
As we recount the world's mishaps.
For in the warmth of family glow,
We find the love that starts to grow.

The Magic of Midwinter

The snow is falling, oh what a thrill,
But Dad's stuck burning down the hill.
With arms outstretched like birds in flight,
He tumbles down, what a silly sight!

The snowmen rise with veggies for noses,
While we throw snowballs, making poses.
"Sledding's easy!" says my wise sis,
As down she zooms, gets lost in bliss.

Hot soup awaits in steaming bowls,
While winter chills dig at our soles.
We dip our toes, sing funny tunes,
As snowy winds dance under the moons.

The magic's here, so pure and bright,
With laughter filling the frosty night.
So here's to joy that won't fade away,
The magic of winter is here to stay!

The Beauty of Laughter's Echo

In a world where giggles bloom,
A silly joke can chase the gloom.
From tickles to snorts, we're all in sync,
Laughter's the magic, don't you think?

With every chuckle, hardly a frown,
We gather cheer like a big, warm gown.
Falling off chairs, who needs a show?
Life's better when we let it flow!

Like bubbles that burst with each silly sound,
In the garden of humor, joy is found.
So let's dance like twinkle lights on a tree,
In the beauty of laughter, we all feel free!

The echo of joy, it travels far,
From the coffee shop to a lively bar.
Let's sing like squirrels in a grand parade,
In laughter's arms, our worries fade!

Joyous Moments Wrapped in Love

Cuddles and chuckles, a perfect blend,
Wrapped in warmth that will never end.
With every hug and silly face,
Love's joyful moments find their place.

Through pancake-flipping and playful chats,
We trade secrets like chubby cats.
Every laugh like a cozy embrace,
In our hearts, there's a special space.

Painted smiles and funny memes,
Love dances lightly on sunny beams.
In this chaos, we find our beat,
Joyous moments are truly sweet!

So let's toast to puns and mischief galore,
Each crazy moment leaves us wanting more.
With love in the air, let's make it clear,
Together we're foolish, delightful, and dear!

Echoes of Wishes Carried by the Wind

Whispers of dreams take flight like kites,
Carried above on breezy nights.
Each wish a giggle, floating high,
Sailing through clouds, we let them fly.

Wishing for pizza or maybe a nap,
Dreams tangled up in a cozy wrap.
With the wind as our giggling friend,
We chase happiness around the bend.

Echoes of wishes tickle the trees,
Swaying gently, like playful bees.
Laughter wraps round like the warmest cap,
In the dance of the breeze, let's take a lap!

So toss your wishes into the blue,
For laughter's the currency, it's true!
On this windy path, we create delight,
With echoes of joy, we take flight!

Laughter Dancing on Icy Paths

Slippery sidewalks, oh what a sight,
A slide and a fall, then laughter takes flight!
With every stumble, a story unfolds,
Where the heart of winter, pure joy holds.

In fluffy parkas, we waddle around,
Chasing each other, the best kind of sound.
As snowflakes sparkle and giggles ignite,
Laughter dances, keeping spirits bright.

Falling like penguins, what a grand show,
Who needs to skate when you can just go?
We twirl and we whirl, no worries, no cares,
On icy paths, we're bold, we're rare!

So grab your mittens, come join the fun,
In a world where laughter's never done.
With hearts so warm on these chilly days,
Let's dance on the ice, in a joyful haze!